THE DOMINIE WORLD OF BIRDS

# Where Birds Are Found



GRAHAM MEADOWS & CLAIRE VIAL

## Contents



DOMINIE PRESS
Pearson Learning Group

# Introduction

Birds are found on every island and on all the **continents** in the world, even **Antarctica**. Most continents have several different types of **habitats**. These habitats can range from deserts to **tropical** rain forests, and from seashores to mountaintops.

Individual **species** of birds are usually found in only one type of habitat. Some species are found in more than one type of habitat. The greatest number of bird species are found in the tropical regions, especially in tropical rain forests.

***Coastal habitat***

***Little blue penguins are indigenous, or native, to Australia and New Zealand.***

***Habitats (clockwise): mountains, deserts, wetlands, and grasslands***

Ocean habitat

Albatrosses are called ocean wanderers.

# Oceans

Oceans cover more than three-quarters of the Earth's surface. They provide food for many different types of animals, including birds.

Birds that spend most of their lives at sea are commonly called seabirds. Many seabirds spend most of their lives far out at sea. They return to land only to nest and raise their young.

Gannets spend much of their lives at sea, but unlike albatrosses and puffins, they usually stay close to the coast. Sometimes they rest and sleep on the water. They nest and raise their young in **colonies** on cliffs or islands.

*Horned puffin on a nest*

*Gannets nesting in a colony*

Coastal habitat

Pied stilts in mangroves

# Coasts

Coasts feature many types of habitats. These habitats include the seashore with its beaches, rocks, and **tide pools**, which are areas on rocks by the ocean that are filled with seawater. Above the high **tide** mark are sand dunes and cliffs.

Many birds, such as gulls and waders, live on or near the seashore. They are commonly called shore birds. When the tide goes out, waders, such as oystercatchers, feed on **invertebrates** that live beneath the seaweed, sand, or mud.

Gulls are commonly seen on beaches. They can also be found far inland, even in cities.

Variable oystercatcher

***Red-billed seagulls on a beach***

***This red-billed seagull is scavenging food from a café table.***

# Freshwater Habitats

Freshwater habitats include **marshes**, streams, **wetlands**, lakes, and rivers. Birds that live in these habitats spend most of their lives on or near fresh water.

***Crowned cranes and an Egyptian goose feeding in a wetland.***

***Egyptian goose standing in a stream***

***Andean flamingo***

Ducks, geese, and swans on a lake

African pygmy geese

Australian pelicans on a lagoon

Grass owl

Secretary bird

# Grasslands and Plains

Grasslands are large open areas covered by grass. They are more or less flat, and may have small groups of shrubs or trees. In Europe and Asia, grasslands are called steppes. In North America, they are called prairies. In the more tropical areas of Africa and South America, they are called savannas.

Some birds, such as ostriches, spend most of their lives on grasslands and plains.

Female ostrich

*Female and male ostriches*

Woodland habitat

# Woodlands

Woodlands are areas covered by trees that are usually less than thirty feet tall. The trees are usually spaced widely apart. Grasses and other small plants grow beneath the trees.

In spring and summer, woodlands provide plenty of food and nesting places for many species of birds.

Great tit

European robin

Bridled titmouse

Deciduous and evergreen forest habitat

Eastern yellow robin

# Temperate Forests

**Temperate** forests grow in regions where there is a big difference between winter and summer temperatures. The tallest trees can be about 100 feet high.

There are two main types of temperate forests. Evergreen forests contain trees that do not lose their leaves in winter. **Deciduous** forests contain trees that lose their leaves in winter. The eastern yellow robin is found in evergreen forests, while the bridled titmouse is found in deciduous forests.

# Tropical Forests

Tropical forests grow in the tropics, in regions where it is warm and damp throughout the year. Plants grow fast in the warm, damp, tropical conditions. In just a few years, a tree can grow to a height of eighty feet.

The tallest trees in these forests can be about 250 feet high. Beneath these tall trees are smaller trees, such as palms, and other plants, such as vines and ferns. In many areas of a tropical forest, these plants grow very close together.

***Tropical forest habitat***

***Purple-throated fruit crow***

*Blue-and-yellow macaw*

*Rainbow lorikeet*

Mountain habitat

# Mountains

There are mountains in many parts of the world. Some mountains are in hot climates, such as the tropics. Others are in cold climates, such as in Antarctica. Depending on where they are, mountain habitats can range from dense forests to snow-covered rocks.

Many bird species spend the summer months high up in the mountains. They move to lower altitudes, where it is warmer, during winter.

*Andean condor*

*Rock wren*

Chestnut-bellied sandgrouse in the desert

Desert habitat

# Deserts

Deserts are very dry places where hardly any rain falls. Very few, if any, plants can grow in a desert habitat. This makes it difficult for birds to find enough food to eat. Despite the **scarcity** of food, some birds have **adapted** to life in the desert.

Cactus wren

# Polar Regions

The **Arctic** region and the continent of Antarctica are the coldest places on Earth. Only a few birds, such as the ivory gull, live in the ice-covered Arctic throughout the year.

To the south of the Arctic is the **tundra**, where the snow and ice melt during the short summer. Here only lichens, mosses, and small shrubs grow. In spring and summer, many birds **migrate** north to the tundra to nest and raise their young. They fly south again before winter.

Only two species of birds live in Antarctica all year, the emperor penguin and the Adélie penguin. Many other birds spend the short summer in Antarctica. They fly north again before winter.

***Snow bunting on the tundra***

***Emperor penguins in Antarctica***

*Ivory gulls in the Arctic*

Indian ring-necked pheasant

# Farmlands

Farmland areas include ground that is being farmed by humans. Much of it is made up of fields divided by hedges or fences. Some farmland areas are used to grow crops, such as wheat. Other areas are used to graze cattle and sheep. Some farmers grow vegetable crops, such as potatoes. Others grow fruit crops, such as apples and grapes.

Many birds have adapted to living in farmland areas. They nest in hedges or trees or on the ground. Some of these birds feed on farmers' crops, and may even become pests.

Cattle egrets are often seen around cattle. They feed on invertebrates that are disturbed by the cattle.

***Blackbird feeding on fallen apples in an orchard***

*Cattle egrets*

*Male blackbird with its chicks*

*Jay drinking at a birdbath*

# Towns and Cities

Many birds have adapted to living in habitats shaped by humans. These can include backyards and gardens, streets, parks, and buildings.

Buildings provide safe places for many birds to nest and raise their young.

Some birds, such as house martins and swallows, build mud nests under the eaves of roofs.

Other birds, such as kittiwakes, nest on the ledges of buildings.

Many people enjoy watching and feeding birds. Some people put out feeders in their backyards to attract birds, especially in winter when the birds' natural food supply is scarce.

Some people put out special nest boxes where birds can nest and raise their young.

***Blue tit on a bird feeder***

*Brown pelicans and Heermann's gulls at a marina*

*House martin at its mud nest*

*Kittiwakes nesting on a building ledge*

# Glossary

**adapted**: Having made gradual physical changes or adjustments over time in order to survive in a particular environment, even under severe conditions

**Antarctica**: A largely uninhabited continent surrounding the South Pole

**Arctic**: The cold, barren region surrounding the North Pole

**colonies**: Groups of animals of the same kind that live together

**continents**: The largest land masses on Earth; there are seven continents—Africa, Antarctica, Asia, Australia, Europe, North America, and South America

**deciduous**: Describing trees and shrubs that shed their leaves seasonally

**habitats**: The places where animals and plants live and grow

**invertebrates**: Animals that do not have a backbone

**marshes**: Areas of low-lying, water-logged land that are poorly drained, difficult to cross on foot, and unfit for agriculture or building

**migrate**: To move from one region or habitat to another in response to cyclical seasonal changes

**scarcity**: An insufficient supply of something

**species**: A group of animals or plants that have many physical characteristics in common

**temperate**: Mild; marked by a moderate climate

**tide**: The rising and falling of the surface of the ocean that occurs twice a day and is caused by the gravitational pull of the Sun and Moon

**tide pools**: Areas of rocks near the ocean that are filled with seawater twice a day when the tide washes over them

**tropical**: Describing areas of land or sea that are very warm throughout the year and lie between the tropic of Capricorn and the tropic of Cancer

**tundra**: Level or rolling treeless plains with a permanently frozen subsoil

**wetlands**: Marshes, swamps, or other areas of land where the soil near the surface is saturated or covered with water, often forming an ideal habitat for a variety of wildlife

# Index